A Second Chance

A Second Chance

An Inspirational Journey
Through the Eyes of an Animal Shelter Volunteer

LIZ MIESNIK

A Second Chance
An Inspirational Journey Through The Eyes of an Animal Shelter Volunteer

Liz Miesnik

ISBN: 978-1-939288-79-0
Library of Congress Control Number: 2014949251

©2014 Liz Miesnik.
All rights reserved.

PLEASE NOTE: In an effort to be more cost efficient and Eco-friendly, we have printed our book on matte paper. Minor anomalies may be noted on some photographs, but this adds to the uniqueness of each printing

Published by A Second Chance Media,
An Imprint of Wyatt-MacKenzie

asecondchancemedia.com

LIZ MIESNIK

Dedication

This book is dedicated to all the volunteers, staff, foster families, donors, adopters and supporters of animal rescues.

Your dedication to the well-being of these animals and the love you show is immeasurable.

"The greatness of a nation and its moral progress can be judged by the way its animals are treated"

Mahatma Gandhi

Table of Contents

Introduction viii

A Second Chance 11

About the Rescues 196

Acknowledgements 203

Introduction

This book was created to inspire, a look through the eyes of a volunteer at a local non-profit animal shelter, to let you see what I see and what is in the eyes of the animals that are here. This book was not intended to be depressing, but on the contrary, to inspire and motivate you. You can make a difference, we all have the ability, it just takes the belief that you can. You will see it in the photos of the volunteers, staff, foster families and others who give their time and love to make a difference. You will see it in the faces of the dogs and cats in their care.

I volunteer at the Humane Society of Eastern Carolina. I see the day-to-day interactions that the staff and volunteers have with these animals and it warms the heart. Knowing that other rescues in our state are facing the same issues as we are, I decided to visit a few of them and include them in this book. Their heartwarming stories of the animals in their care and hopes for the future of their cause are truly inspirational.

Some of the animals depicted in this book are still waiting to be adopted. You may find out more about these pets and the organizations that care for them at the end of the book.

Yes, it all starts with you; you can make a difference in the lives of these animals, it just takes a minute to open your heart. Part of the proceeds of this book will be given back to the rescues and facilities represented in this book. I thank you and they thank you.

Until they find their forever home...

LIZ MIESNIK
x

"The hardest thing to give away is kindness;

It always comes back to you"

English Proverb

"I alone can't change the world,

but I can cast a stone across the waters

to create many ripples"

Mother Teresa

Bear

A SECOND CHANCE

LIZ MIESNIK

"Change the way you look at things,

and the things you look at will change"

Buddhist Proverb

"To accomplish great things we must not only act, but also dream, not only plan, but also believe"

Anatole France

A SECOND CHANCE

Hope

"Until he extends the circle of compassion

to all living things, man will

not himself find peace"

Albert Schweitzer

"There are two ways to spread the light:

To be the candle

or the mirror that reflects it"

Edith Wharton

April

Belle

LIZ MIESNIK

"You gain strength, courage and confidence by every experience in which you really stop to look fear in the face. You are able to say to you 'I lived through this horror. I can take the next thing that comes along'.
You must do the things you think you cannot do"

Eleanor Roosevelt

"Don't be afraid to be unique or speak your mind because that's what makes you different from everyone else"

Dave Thomas

Nicole

Carly

"Love many things, for therein lies true strength and whosoever loves much performs much, and can accomplish much, and what is done in love is done well"

      Vincent Van Gogh

"The magic begins in you. Feel your own energy and realize similar energy exists within the Earth, stones, plants, water, wind, fire, colors and animals"

Scott Cunningham

A SECOND CHANCE

Axelia

LIZ MIESNIK

"Surround yourself with the dreamers and the doers,

the believers and the thinkers.

But most of all surround yourself with those who see the

greatness within you, even when you

don't see it in yourself"

Unknown

"When you are inspired by some great purpose, some extraordinary project, all your thoughts break their bonds. Your mind transcends limitations, your consciousness in every direction, and you find yourself in a new, great and wonderful world. Dormant forces, faculties and talents become alive, and you discover yourself to be a greater person by far than you ever dreamed yourself to be"

Patanjali

A SECOND CHANCE

LIZ MIESNIK

"Compassion is our deepest nature.

It arises from our interconnection with all things"

Buddhist Proverb

"Follow your Bliss…

and the Universe will open doors

where there were only walls"

Joseph Campbell

Spirit

A SECOND CHANCE

LIZ MIESNIK

"Always do right.

This will gratify some people,

and astonish the rest"

Mark Twain

"Most people who succeed in the face of seemingly impossible conditions are people who simply don't know how to quit"

Robert Schuler

A SECOND CHANCE

LIZ MIESNIK

"Too often we under estimate the power

of a touch, a smile, a kind word, a listening ear,

an honest compliment or the smallest act of caring,

all of which have the potential to turn a life around…"

Leo Buscaglia

"Most of the important things in the world have been accomplished by people who have kept on trying when there seemed to be no hope at all"

Dale Carnegie

A SECOND CHANCE

LIZ MIESNIK

"Act as if what you do makes a difference. It does…"

William James

"A journey of a thousand miles....
begins with a single step"

Taoist Proverb

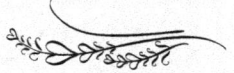

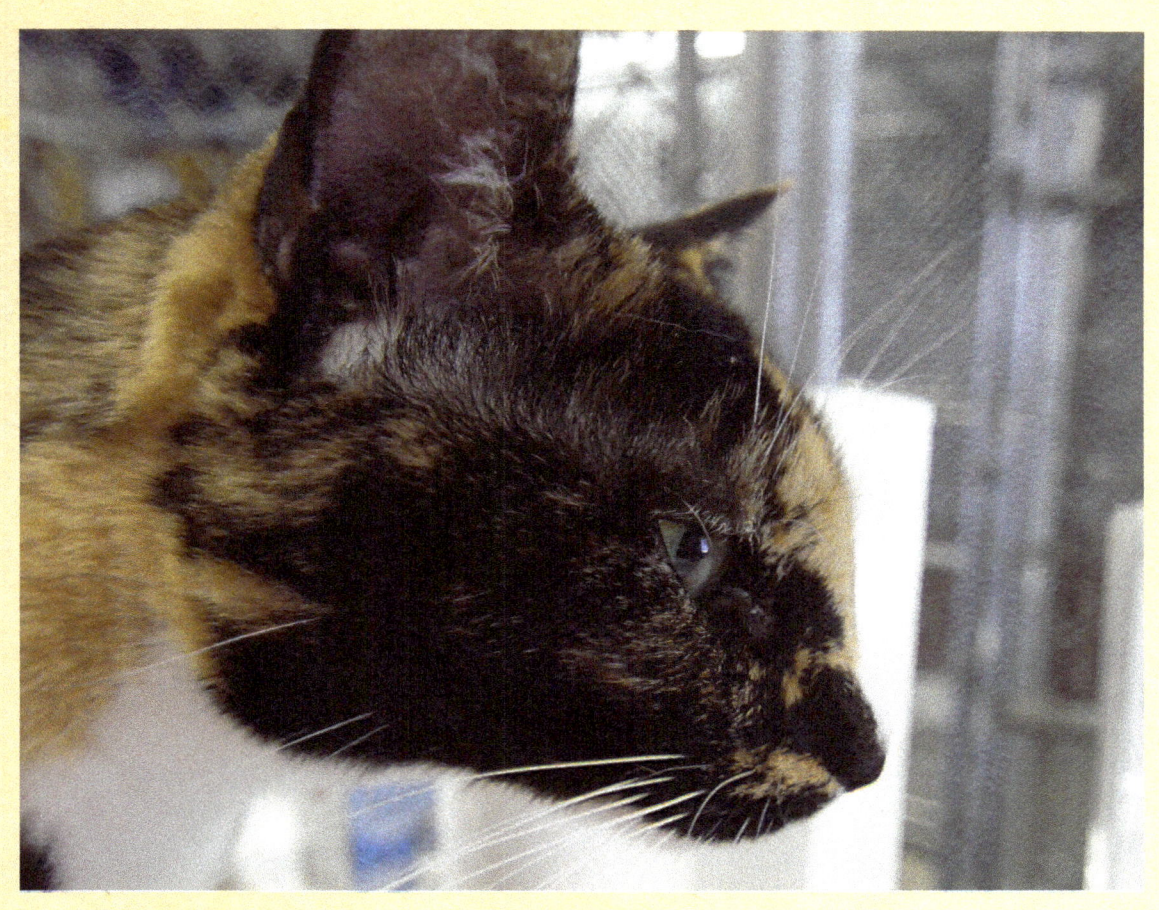

Jackie

LIZ MIESNIK

"What we are today comes from our thoughts of yesterday. And our present thoughts, build our life of tomorrow. Our life is the creation of our mind"

Buddha

"Until one has loved an animal, a part of one's soul remains un-awakened"

Anatole France

A SECOND CHANCE

LIZ MIESNIK

"From small beginnings come great things"

American Proverb

"Don't only practice your art, but force

your way into its secrets,

for it and knowledge can rise

men to the Divine"

Ludwig Van Beethoven

Tuck

A SECOND CHANCE

Fonzie

LIZ MIESNIK

"Every time you smile at someone,

it is an action of love,

a gift to that person,

a beautiful thing"

Mother Teresa

"Change is an attitude of mind and the place to start is within ourselves"

John Harvey-Jones

A SECOND CHANCE

Merlot

LIZ MIESNIK

"Keep away from people who try to belittle your ambitions. Small people always do that, but the really great make you feel that you, too, can become great"

Mark Twain

"Those that bring sunshine to the lives

of others cannot keep it

from themselves"

James Matthew Barrie

Gus

A SECOND CHANCE

LIZ MIESNIK

"The future belongs to those who believe in the beauty of their dreams"

Eleanor Roosevelt

"Leave the world a better place than you found it"

Robert Baden-Powell

Sam

A SECOND CHANCE

LIZ MIESNIK

"Learn to get in touch with the silence within yourself,

and know that everything in this life

has a purpose…"

Elisabeth Kuber-Ross

"You should be the change

you want to see in the world"

Mahatma Gandhi

A SECOND CHANCE

LIZ MIESNIK

"One's philosophy is not best expressed in words;
It is expressed in the choices one makes.
In the long run, we shape our lives
and we shape ourselves.
The process never ends until we die.
And, the choices we make are ultimately
our own responsibility"

Eleanor Roosevelt

"A thing of beauty is a joy forever; its loveliness increases; it will never pass into nothingness"

John Keats

Junior

A SECOND CHANCE

Hank

LIZ MIESNIK

"Courage is the first of human qualities because it is the quality which guarantees all others"

Winston Churchill

"A friend is someone who knows the song in your heart and can sing it back to you when you have forgotten the words"

Unknown

A SECOND CHANCE

Crush

LIZ MIESNIK

"It is never too late

to become what you might have been"

George Elliot

"The Universe is change; our life is what our thoughts make it"

Marcus Aurelius

Marley

A SECOND CHANCE

LIZ MIESNIK

*"To understand the heart and mind of a person,
look not at what he has already achieved,
but at what he aspires to"*

Kahil Gibran

"The best and most beautiful things in the world

cannot be seen or even touched.

They must be felt with the heart"

Helen Keller

Gordon

A SECOND CHANCE

LIZ MIESNIK

"Love is an element which though physically unseen, is as real as air or water. It is an acting, living, moving force... it moves in waves and currents like those of the ocean"

Prentice Mulford

"Dream lofty dreams,

and as you dream...

so you shall become"

John Ruskin

A SECOND CHANCE

LIZ MIESNIK

"When you see beauty in all things, you will not only find it, you will become it"

Unknown

"When you realize there is nothing lacking,

the whole world belongs to you"

Lao Tzu

Jack Frost

A SECOND CHANCE

LIZ MIESNIK

"There are many things in life that will catch your eye,

but only a few will catch your heart...

Pursue those..."

Unknown

"The person who sends out positive thoughts, activates the world around him positively, and draws back to him, positive results"

Norman Vincent Peale

A SECOND CHANCE

LIZ MIESNIK

"You already possess everything necessary to become great"

Native American Proverb, Crow

"Love and compassion are necessities, not luxuries. Without them, humanity cannot survive"

Buddha

Kiki

A SECOND CHANCE

Dobie

LIZ MIESNIK

*"See with your mind,
hear with your heart"*

Kurdish Proverb

"Everyone thinks of changing the world, but no one thinks of changing himself".

Tolstoy

A SECOND CHANCE

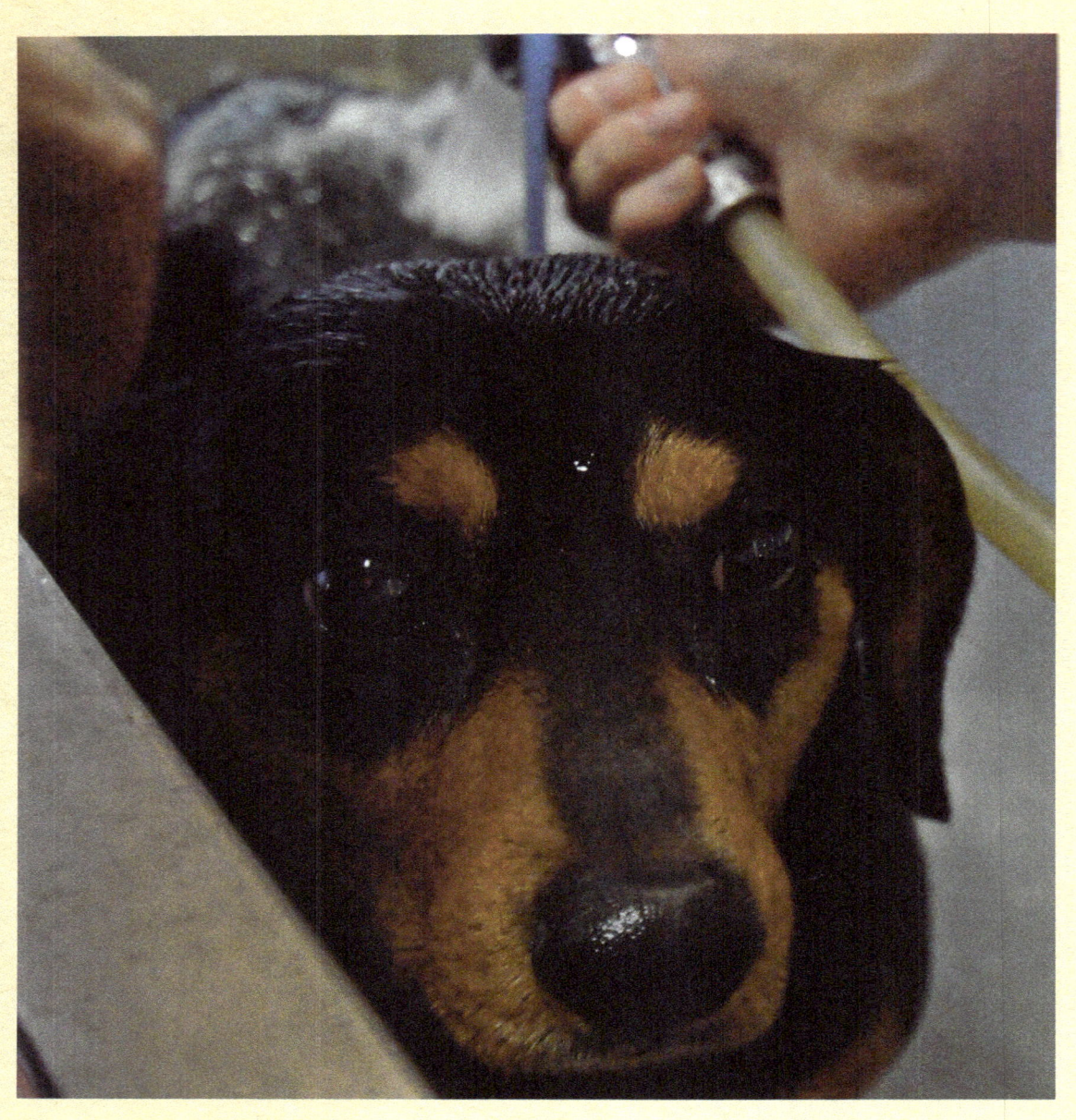

LIZ MIESNIK

"Success is measured not so much by the position that one has reached in life as by the obstacles which one has overcome while trying to succeed"

Booker T. Washington

"The new source of power is not money in the hands of few, but information in the hands of many"

W.W. Rostow

Scooby

A SECOND CHANCE

Splotch

LIZ MIESNIK

"Imagination is more important than knowledge. For knowledge is limited, whereas imagination embraces the entire world, stimulating progress, giving birth to evolution"

Albert Einstein

"Kind words can be short and easy to speak, but their echoes are truly endless"

Mother Teresa

Lassie

A SECOND CHANCE

LIZ MIESNIK

"Regardless of who you are, or where you have been, you can be what you want to be"

W. Clement Stone

"People do not decide to become extraordinary. They decide to accomplish extraordinary things"

Edmond Hillary

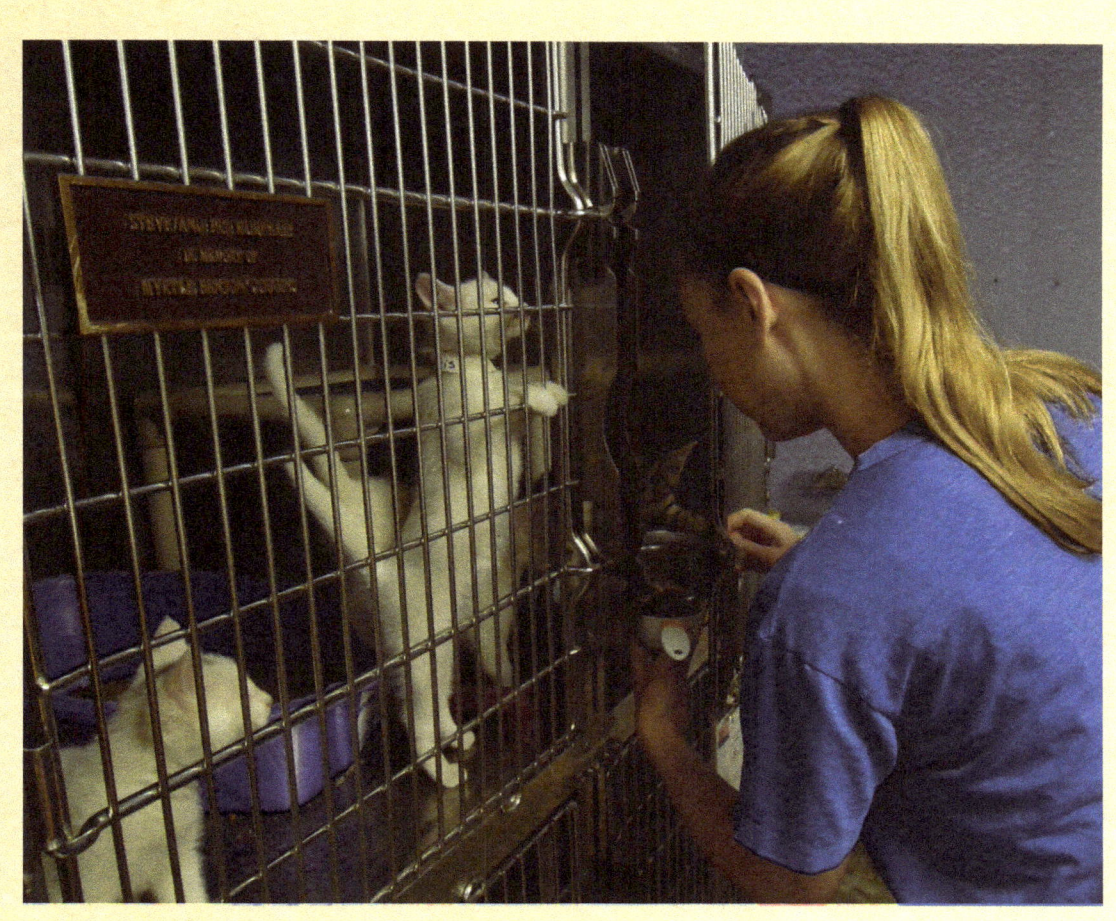

A SECOND CHANCE

"Every thought you produce, anything you say, any action you do, it bears your signature"

Thich Nhat Hanh

"The soul is the same in all living creatures, although the body of each is different"

Hippocrates

A SECOND CHANCE

Spencer

LIZ MIESNIK

"Nurture your mind with great thoughts, for you will never go any higher...than you think"

Benjamin Disraeli

"A generous heart, kind speech and compassion are the things which renew Humanity"

Buddha

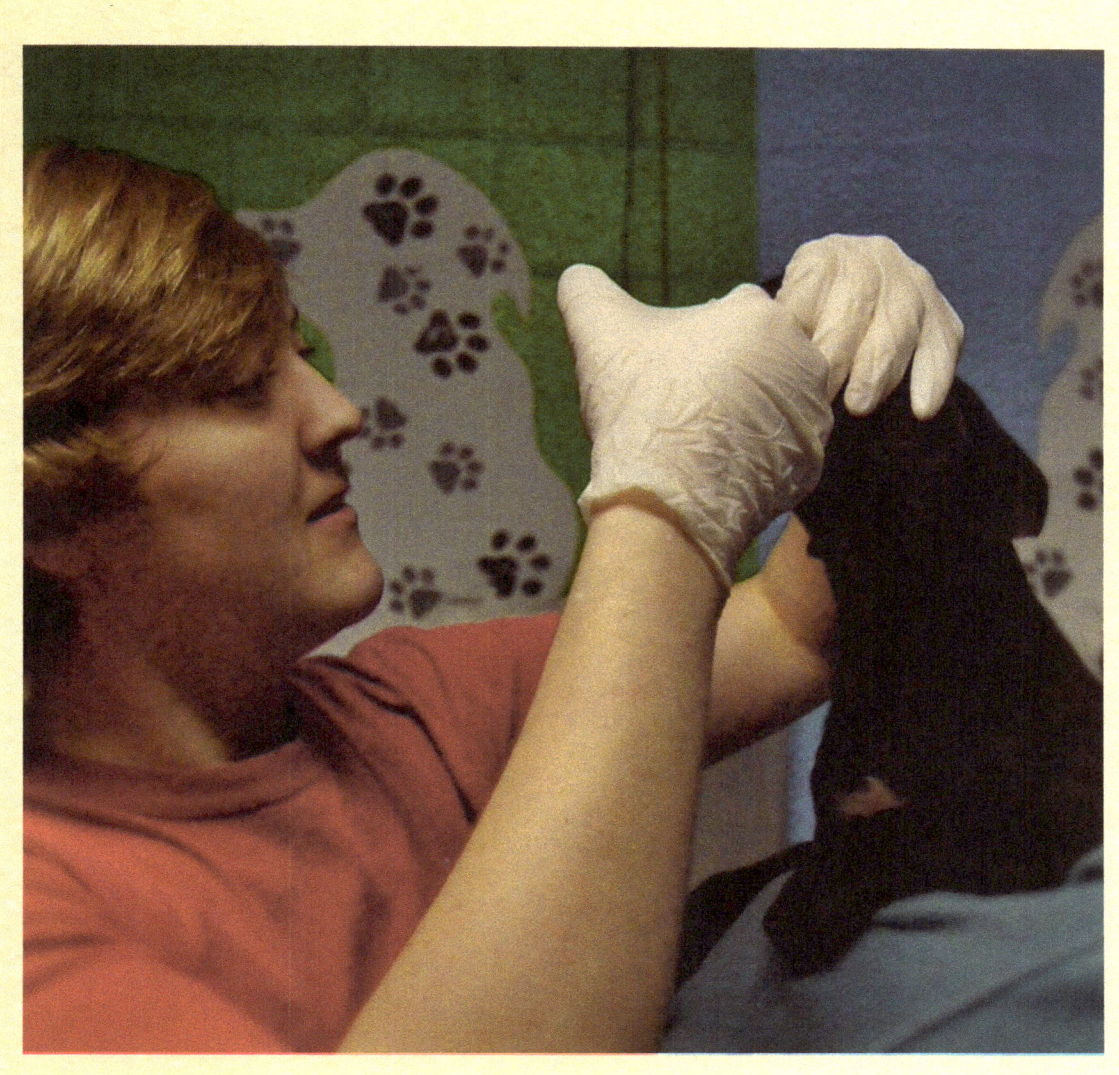

A SECOND CHANCE

LIZ MIESNIK

"Once you make a decision, the Universe conspires to make it happen"

Ralph Waldo Emerson

"What the mind of man can conceive and believe, the mind of man can achieve"

Napoleon Hill

Maggie

A SECOND CHANCE

Valentine

LIZ MIESNIK

"Success is liking yourself, liking what you do, and liking how you do it"

Maya Angelou

"The ultimate measure of a man is not where he stands in moments of comfort and convenience, but where he stands at times of challenge and controversy"

Martin Luther King, Jr.

A SECOND CHANCE

Buster

LIZ MIESNIK

"Remember, a person who wins success may have been counted out many times before he wins because he refuses to give up"

Kemmons Wilson

"Love...it surrounds every being and extends slowly to embrace all that shall be"

Khalil Gibran

A SECOND CHANCE

Allie

LIZ MIESNIK

"I have looked into your eyes with my eyes.

I have put my heart near your heart"

Pope John XXIII

"All that we are is a result of what we have thought. The mind is everything. What we think we become"

Buddha

A SECOND CHANCE

Buddy

LIZ MIESNIK

"Nothing great was ever achieved without enthusiasm"

Ralph Waldo Emerson

"Our smile affirms our awareness and
determination to live in peace and joy.
The source of a true smile is an awakened mind"

Thick Nhat Hanh

A SECOND CHANCE

Mama Laura

LIZ MIESNIK

"Change is an attitude of mind and the place to start is within ourselves"

Harvey Jones

"Great hearts steadily send forth the secret forces that incessantly draw great events"

Ralph Waldo Emerson

A SECOND CHANCE

Otto

LIZ MIESNIK

"If something comes to life in others because of you, than you have made an approach to immortality"

Norman Cousins

"The more you like yourself,

the less you are like anyone else,

which makes you unique"

Walt Disney

A SECOND CHANCE

LIZ MIESNIK

"The miracle is not to walk on water. The miracle is to walk on the green earth in the present moment, to appreciate the peace and beauty that are available now"

Thich Nhat Hanh

"You can have anything you want if you want it badly enough. You can be anything you want to be, do anything you set out to accomplish, if you hold that desire with singleness and purpose"

Abraham Lincoln

Lucy

A SECOND CHANCE

LIZ MIESNIK

"We are all one child spinning through Mother Sky"

Native American Proverb, Shawnee

"The Journey is the Reward"

Taoist Proverb

A SECOND CHANCE

LIZ MIESNIK

"Everything in the universe has rhythm,

everything dances"

Maya Angelou

A SECOND CHANCE

"Occasionally in life there are those moments of unutterable fulfillment which cannot be completely explained by those symbols called words. Their meanings can only be articulated by the inaudible language of the heart"

Martin Luther King, Jr.

A SECOND CHANCE

LIZ MIESNIK

"It's not how much you do, but how much love you put into the doing that matters"

Mother Teresa

"Happiness does not depend on what you have or who your are… it solely relies on what you think"

Buddha

A SECOND CHANCE

LIZ MIESNIK

"You are not what you think you are.

But, what you think…you are"

Norman Vincent Peale

"Thought is the sculptor who can create the person you want to be"

Henry David Thoreau

A SECOND CHANCE

Stars

LIZ MIESNIK

"It is not enough to be compassionate.

You must act also"

Taoist Proverb

"Compassion for animals is intimately associated with goodness of character, and it may be confidently asserted that he who is cruel to animals cannot be a good man"

Arthur Schopenhauer

A SECOND CHANCE

LIZ MIESNIK

"A dog is the only thing on earth that loves you more than he loves himself"

Josh Billings

"Don't wait. The time will never be just right. Start where you stand and work with whatever tools you may have at your command and better tools will be found as you go along"

Napoleon Hill

A SECOND CHANCE

Layla

LIZ MIESNIK

"Thousands of candles can be lighted by a single candle, and the life of the candle will not be shortened. Happiness never decreases by being shared"

Buddha

"Trust yourself. Create the kind of self that you will be happy to live with all of your life. Make the most of yourself by fanning the tiny, inner sparks of possibility into flames of achievement"

Golda Meir

A SECOND CHANCE

LIZ MIESNIK

"There is a supreme power and ruling force which pervades and rules the boundless Universe. You are a part of this power"

Prentice Mulford

"Throw your heart over the fence and the rest will follow"

Norman Vincent Peale

A SECOND CHANCE

LIZ MIESNIK

"The intellect has little to do on the road to discovery. There comes a leap in consciousness, call it intuition or what you will, and the solution comes to you and you don't know how or why"

Albert Einstein

About The Rescues

In every community there are homeless animals. In the US, there are an estimated 6-8 million homeless animals entering shelters every year[1]. Unfortunately, barely half of these animals are adopted. Each year, about 2.7 million healthy, adoptable cats and dogs — about one every 11 seconds — are euthanized in the U.S.[2]

Working together, we can make a difference in these numbers. How, you may ask?

Education: Educating the public on spaying and neutering their pets, training to reduce unwanted behavior and pet health and vaccinations

Spaying and neutering your pet is the only 100% permanently effective method of birth control for dogs and cats. Not only will this prevent over-breeding and unwanted litters; but it also has health benefits for both cats and dogs. A *USA Today* (May 7, 2013) article cites that pets that live in states with the highest rates of spaying and neutering also live the longest. Spaying and neutering may also cut down the risk for certain cancers in both cats and dogs.

Another way is through education on training to reduce unwanted behaviors, thus reducing owner surrenders for behavioral issues.

Many shelters offer discounts for training through sponsors if you adopt through the facility. They know that training the animal as well as the owner is crucial for a happy existence.

Visit your veterinarian regularly to keep up to date on your pet's vaccines and health issues. Behavior issues can be a direct result of an underlying health issue.

Being involved and raising awareness is the key to helping these animals. Spread the word about spaying and neutering, adopt your pet from a shelter or rescue group, volunteer at your local shelter or raise awareness through community events. Donations of both supplies and money are also important as many of these facilities are 501 C (3) non-profit and rely solely on the funds you donate. Fostering; many of these pets need to be in a foster home, as this helps reduce stress caused by shelter life and helps the pet adjust to a normal home life.

The following pages are a brief description of the rescues featured in this book. These non-profit rescues and facilities rely solely on the funds received from the public. Please remember to give generously to your local non-profit animal rescue or shelter. You can make a difference one life at a time.

---

[1] Humane Society of the United States/ "Why you should spay/neuter your pet"/accessed 5/20/14
http://www.humanesociety.org

[2] Humane Society of the United States/"Pet Overpopulation"/accessed 5/20/14
http://www.humanesociety.org

Until they find their forever home...

S.O.A.R. Southport/Oak Island Animal Rescue
3376 St. Charles Place SE
Southport, NC 28461
910-457-6340
Email – director.soar@gmail.com
www.soar-nc.org

Soar was funded by Jeannine Friday Bicknell in 1992. SOAR is a non-profit; no kill facility located just outside Wilmington North Carolina. The facility is situated on beautiful partially tree covered grounds and has large play areas as well as shady trails to walk the dogs. Unfortunately, they do not have an indoor facility for the dogs at this time, and this is one of the future plans they are working toward.

An enclosed kennel would provide shelter for the dogs during inclement weather during the hot days of summer, the cold days of winter and during Hurricane season. SOAR is a 501 (c)(3) non- profit and relies solely on donations from the public for the funds to keep this facility running.

SOAR also provides 3 separate homes for the feline friends. All three provide open interaction for the cats with inside as well as outside protective areas for them to roam without having to be in a kennel. Kennels are provided for the few who may have issues interacting positively with their other feline friends. One Cattery is strictly for FIV (Feline Immunodeficiency Virus) cats, and one for FeLv(Feline Leukemia Virus), as they need to be separate from other healthy cats.

Humane Society of Eastern Carolina
3520 Tupper Drive
Greenville NC 27834
252-413-7247
Email – HSECgeneral@gmail.com
www.hsecarolina.org

The Humane Society of Eastern Carolina is a no-kill, 501 (c)(3) not for profit organization and relies solely on donations from the public for the funds to keep this facility running. They do not receive any local, state or federal funds, nor they do they receive any funding from the Humane Society of the United States or the ASPCA.

The Humane Society of Eastern Carolina's mission is to serve as a safe haven for homeless and neglected pets and act as a resource to the community. By educating the public about issues pertaining to animals, they can work towards the elimination of over breeding of dogs and cats and teach owners to be responsible pet owners. Every animal adopted is two saved: the one going home and the one coming in. All animals are fully vetted and spayed/neutered prior to leaving the facility.

Ruff Love Rescue and Great Dane Friends of Ruff Love
PO Box 2013
Thomasville, NC 27361
Phone: 704-584-9257
Email - dogs315@northstate.net
www.greatdanefriends.com and www.ruffloverescue.com

Great Dane Friends of Ruff Love was started by a group of volunteers dedicated to saving Danes and other dogs, especially ones that may be passed up by other rescues due to special needs. They are an extension of Ruff Love Rescue based in Thomasville NC. Ruff Love Rescue (RLR) is a non-profit, 501 (c)(3), no-kill dog rescue and foster care organization dedicated to the care of abused, neglected and abandoned dogs. Ruff Love Rescue has worked for over 15 years to place their dogs in safe, loving homes. All dogs with Ruff Love live in private foster homes - they have no facility. RLR is dependent entirely on community donations and fundraisers.

Great Dane Friends is a rescue group that will go as far with medical care as is necessary to restore a dog's quality of life. In addition to the basic vaccines, heartworm tests, and spay/neuters, they often have a greater need for money to help pay for more expensive medical needs. Great Dane Friends relies solely on donations from the public and foster families. They do not have a facility, but home each dog with a foster family that will provide love, companionship and medical care these beautiful dogs will need till they are adopted

Paws Place

Paws Place Dog Rescue
3701 East Boiling Spring Road
Winnabow, NC 28479
910-845-7297
Email – info@pawsplace.org
www.pawsplace.org

Paws Place was founded in 1999 as a no-kill sanctuary dedicated to the rescue, rehabilitation and adoption of dogs. The dog kennels and layout were designed with special attention to the dogs comfort, safety and proper hygiene. Since its inception, Paws Place has found permanent homes for over 1200 dogs. Each dog is vetted upon arrival and will be given rabies shots and started on heartworm prevention, micro chipped and spayed or neutered prior to adoption. Paws Place is a 501 (c)(3) non-profit facility and relies solely on donations and volunteers. Their future plans include an indoor facility for the dogs so during inclement weather, they have a place to be comfortable. Dedicated to finding them loving homes no matter how long it takes. ONE LIFE AT A TIME!

Acknowledgements

First, I would like to thank my husband, Jim, for his patience and acceptance of my love for these animals and the day in and day out involvement and time put forth towards making a change for them. And thank you to my children, Amanda and Zack, for their love and understanding of my mission.

Thank you to Nancy with Wyatt-MacKenzie Publishing for providing me direction, and to Laurie for her editing expertise. Your help gives me the opportunity to make a positive change in the public perception of animal rescue.

Thank you to Steve, Leah and Tony with Paws Place Dog Rescue, to Cathy with Southport/Oak Island Animal Rescue and to Sue with Ruff Love Rescue, as well as their volunteers. Your love and commitment to these animals is an inspiration to us all.

To all the volunteers, staff, foster families, donors, supporters and sponsors of animal rescues everywhere, we could not make it happen without you! Keep up the great work and THANK YOU!

"We must fight against the spirit of unconscious cruelty with which we treat the animals.
Animals suffer as much as we do.
True humanity does not allow us to impose such sufferings on them.
It is our duty to make the whole world recognize it.
Until we extend our circle of compassion to all living things, humanity will not find peace"

Albert Schweitzer

www.ingramcontent.com/pod-product-compliance
Lightning Source LLC
Chambersburg PA
CBHW061124070526
44584CB00033B/4217